Contents

I Killed Him for His Wardrobe Space	2
Not the Elephant	4
I Thought I Tasted Death Today	5
It Really Is a Bugger	6
Warrior Worrier	8
Chocolate Addiction	10
Hyperbolic Warning if Planning an Affair	12
Screen Saver	14
I'm Writing Lines	15
Force Quit	16
Only Kids	17
Slight Trauma for Friends	18
Eenie, Meenie, Miney, Mo	20
Feeling the Chemistry	21
It's Weird How Things Can Affect You	22
Oh Spider!	24
Living with OCDN	25
On Clearing Mum's House	27
Yoga Class	29
Sarah, Our Surprise	31

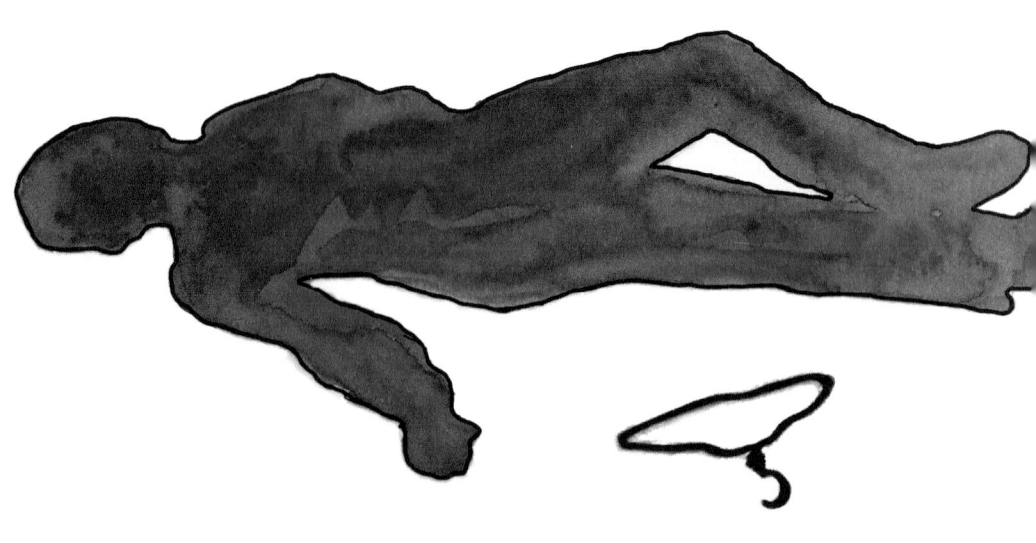

I Killed Him for His Wardrobe Space

I Killed Him for His Wardrobe Space

I killed him for his wardrobe space
Is that a little drastic?
But his attire was tired and dull
Whilst mine alive, fantastic.

There may have been other reasons
That led to this wanton act,
The slurping tea, the noisy wee,
Emotions tight, intact.

Regrets? Remorse? Retribution fears?
No, they've all passed me by,
But I do miss our arguments,
Our tensions, mournful sighs.

The thrill of one-upmanship,
The verbal cut and thrust,
The occasional need for truces,
To reassess, adjust.

I killed him for his wardrobe space,
Is that a little drastic?
But his mind was tired and dull,
Whilst mine iconoclastic.

I Killed Him for His Wardrobe Space

Not the Elephant

Your former love, your illicit affair,
Your transgression, your crush,
Is not the elephant in the room,
She is the room.

Her being, her image, her essence shimmering
Like a mirage,
A flickering black and white film
Across the backdrop of my life.

Her absence is powerful, potent, full of promise,
My presence is predictable, pedestrian, mundane.
She is in your head,
I am in your reality.
She is in your dreams,
And I cannot fight a dream.

I Thought I Tasted Death Today

I thought I tasted death today,
A bitter potion on my lips.
Shadows formed and faded, then,
A darkening, a heart eclipse.
No warning, fleeting, yet no doubt –
This would be death
When death will out.

I thought I tasted death today,
I felt the night time of the soul.
I felt a shiver, felt the gaze,
A life in balance, I waited, crazed.
No warning, fleeting, yet no doubt –
This would be death
When death will out.

It Really Is A Bugger

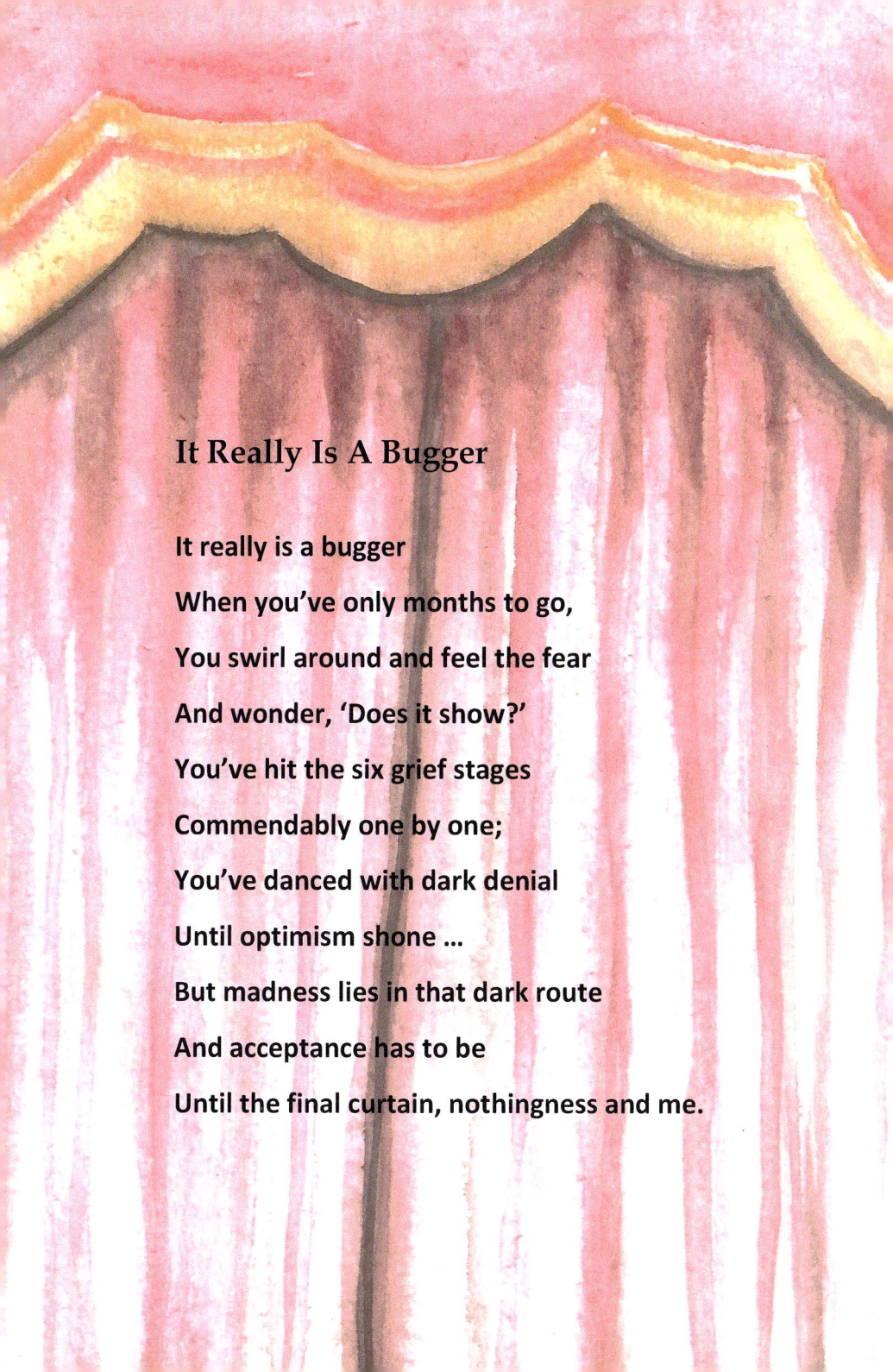

It really is a bugger

When you've only months to go,

You swirl around and feel the fear

And wonder, 'Does it show?'

You've hit the six grief stages

Commendably one by one;

You've danced with dark denial

Until optimism shone …

But madness lies in that dark route

And acceptance has to be

Until the final curtain, nothingness and me.

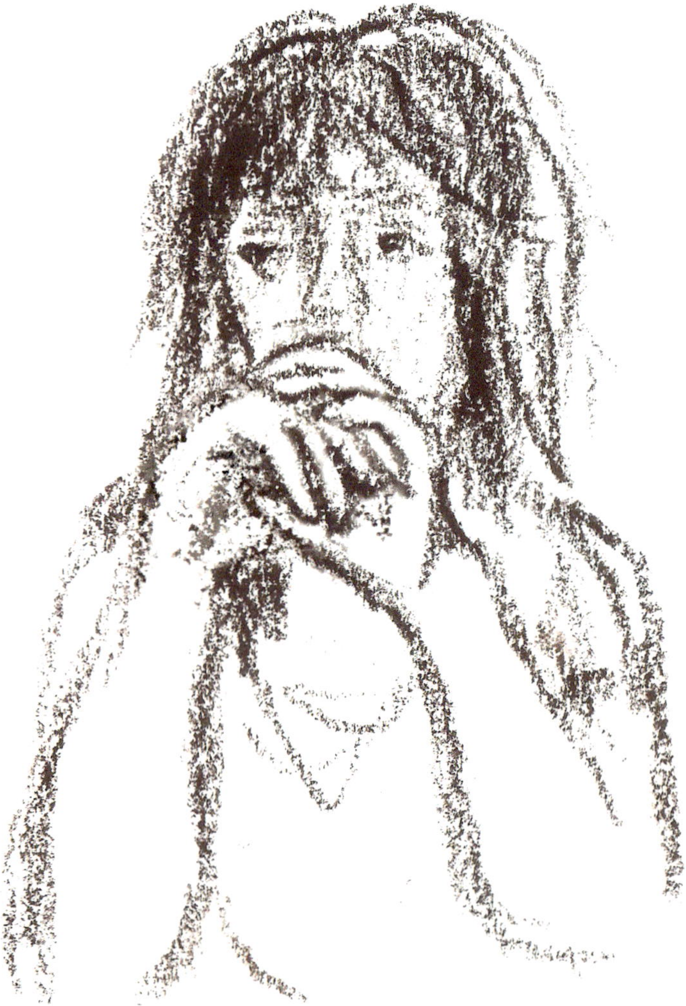

Warrior Worrier

Being in the number one team
Of the Worrier League
My default position is stress;
A Warrior Worrier
Committed, a courier,
With worries to find,
Collect, coalesce.

It's a permanent condition –
Self-diagnosed –
Becoming apparent when one problem goes
And is simply replaced by another.
Son – bullied or bullying? Friendless? Or dead?
Daughter – is she perhaps looking too thin?
Those texting alerts from your partner's phone,
The brain simply won't give in.

And when, much later, all seems resolved
And all the concerns are dispatched,
The Warrior Worrier sighs with relief …
As the next set of worries is hatched.

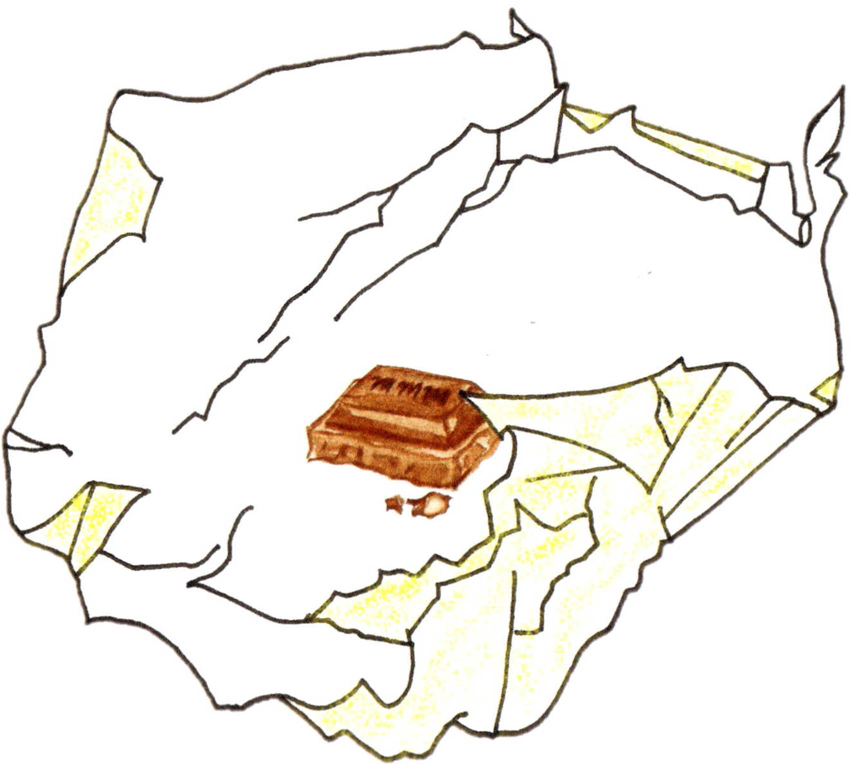

Chocolate Addiction

Chocolate addiction
Chocolate affliction
Chocolate craving, raving, caving
Into temptation
And then ...
Pure elation
Taste sensation
Oral ecstasy.
Savouring each moment
Of stolen, guilty pleasure,
Knowing the denouement
But shrugging it away.
For chocolate is enchantment now,
Compelling and overwhelming
'Til slowly, slowly, chocolate power
Seeps relentlessly away.
So high descending
Pleasure ending
Drug withdrawing
Serotonin yawning
Cold chocolate turkey
Then ...
Guilty reverie.

I Killed Him for His Wardrobe Space

Hyperbolic Warning if Planning an Affair

Remember …

The illicit thrill
The frisson, fever and delight
Will have consequences …
For your toes once dipped in the lake of deceit
Will cause ripples, tides, tsunamis
Until the trembling volcano
Can contain itself no longer and
Spews out its tortuous red anger
And you are subsumed
And your life falls apart …
Hyperbolic warning
If planning an affair.

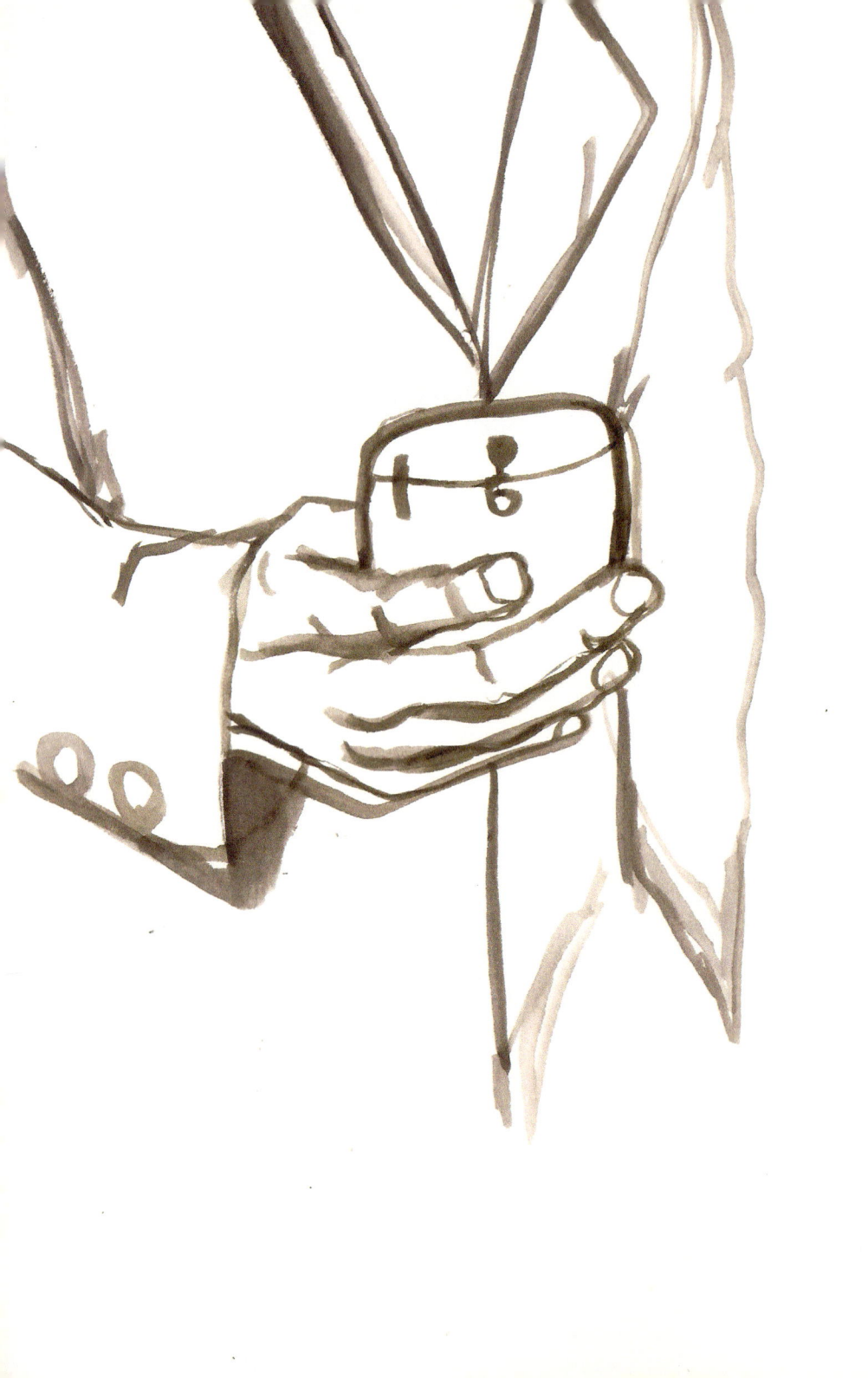

Screen Saver

My photo is your screen-saver,
Your faithful wife and true,
I think I look alluring
What a thoughtful thing to do.

But my geeky friend with geeky son
Seemed cynical and drew
Worrying attention to a well known
Spoof and through

Their expertise and boldness
(and a devious search in trash)
Found Looby-Loo, sans attire,
She really cut a dash …

Now I no longer grace your screen
No longer grace your life,
I've moved in with my best friend
And Looby-Loo's now your wife.

And your screen saver …

I'm Writing Lines

I'm writing lines – it's necessary –
Our teachers used to say.
I'm writing lines – it's therapy –
Takes active thoughts away.

I'm writing lines in a vain attempt
To keep my thoughts becalmed;
Become the scribe, absorb my mind
Meditative, soothing, a balm.

Now my page is almost filled
The die is almost cast
Will it work, like lines at school?
"I must not … keep talking in class."

I finish, sigh, put down my pen,
I sit back, then peruse
The lines, the mantra, I have written:
"I must not … keep thinking of you."

Force Quit

We met online
And I like to think
That as we bonded
Our Macs responded – inline.   **[Save as]**

We moved in together
Our Macs side by side
Tapping in harmony
Our fingers glide – over the keys.   **[Save as]**

We mailed and we shared
Our lives over-lapping:
Our music, our photos, our instagramming,
Never fearing we were nearing trash.   **[Save as]**

Your leaving was sudden, unexpected, fast
And shattered, I gazed at the screen –
A message:
    "Your memory is almost full,
    Here's what you must do to wipe clean.
    Force quit"   **[Force quit]**

Only Kids

Only kids can afford to be smug;

This statement requires no response

It's inherent in their knowledge

Their parents only did it once.

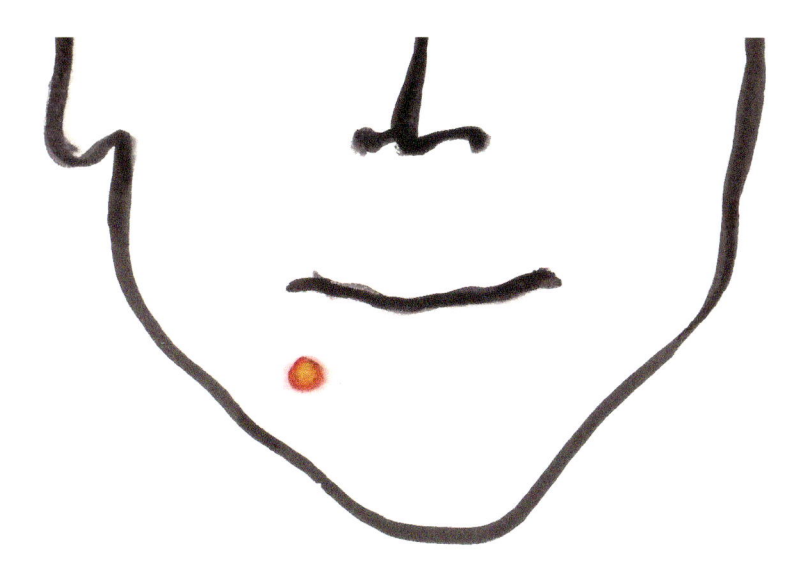

Slight Trauma for Friends

My friend …

Temper your good fortune

With a little local trauma,

For no-one likes perfection undiluted.

When things are going swimmingly

And life seems like a dream,

Let family and work become polluted

By faulty fridge, a failed exam

A spot, a fine, an error,

Such things will make me love you more,

From me … a schadenfreude.

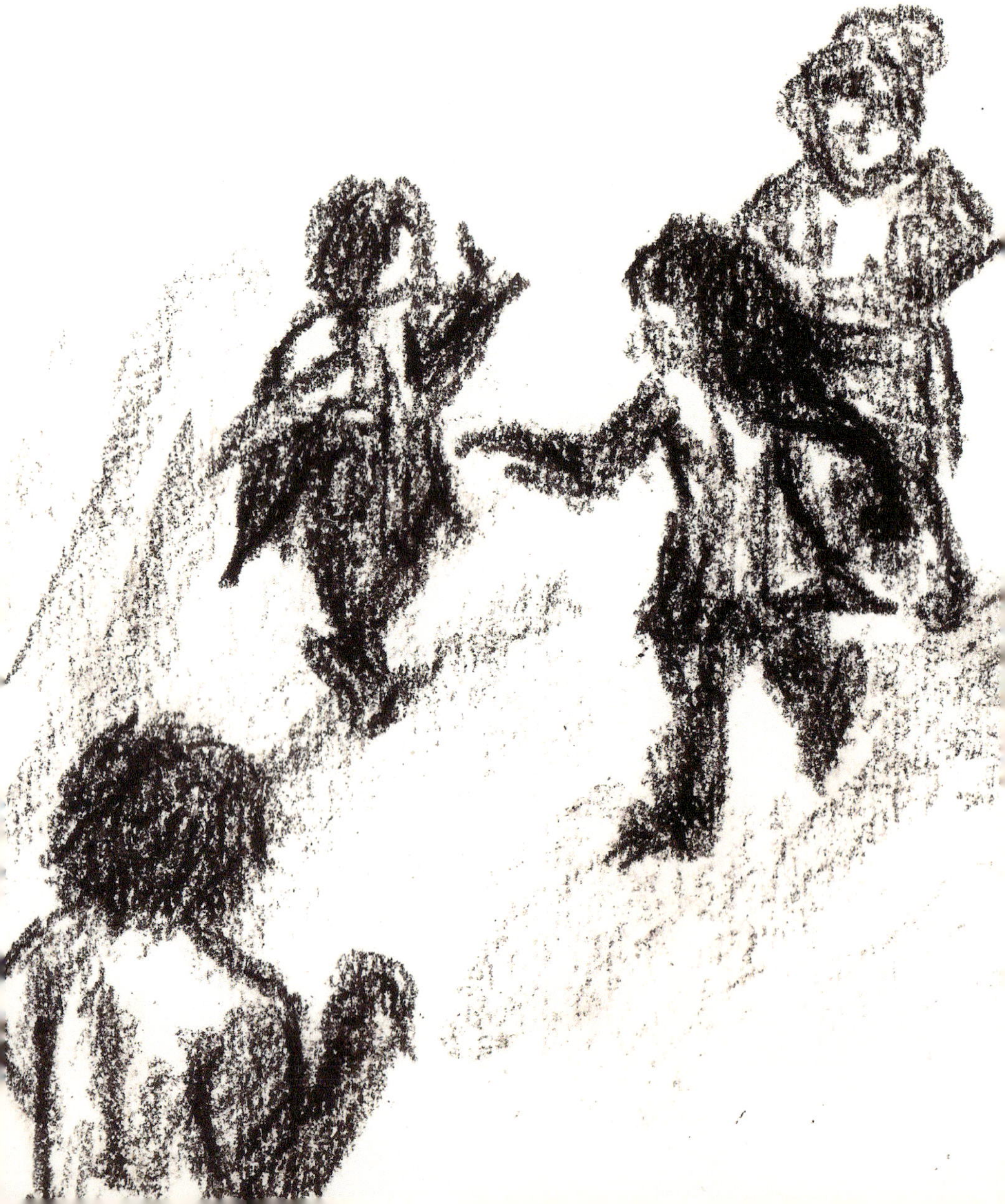

Eenie, Meenie, Miney, Mo

Eenie, Meenie, Miney, Mo
Catch a tiger by the toe,
Playground games you lose or win
Childhood captured in a spin ... of
Fists out, Meenie, Miney, Mo,
Today it's you and, "out you go!"

Introducing apprehension
At sixty plus, increasing tension,
In the consultant's sterile room
Echoes of that childhood tune,
Eenie, Meenie, Miney, Mo
It's terminal and "out you go!"

Feeling the Chemistry

Feeling the chemistry

Experiencing the buzz,

Imagining an electric touch

Dare not think it's lurvv …

Imagination overdrive

Or maybe self-delusion,

Taking steps to minimise

These thoughts and this confusion.

Essential to play it cool,

Assume a careless, nonchalant air,

Take up that worthy hobby

Pretend that you're not there.

Didn't work, so …

Still feeling the chemistry

That enigmatic buzz,

But now I think that possibly, maybe, mmm

It could *just* well be lurvv …

It's Weird How Things Can Affect You

It's weird how things can affect you,
How the prosaic becomes the profound;
Why words can spring unbidden, unguarded
And the poem emerges unbound.
Rough still, unhewn, jagged edges
But at its centre a diamond, a heart,
Born from love or desire or betrayal
No pretence, just release, just a start
Of renewal.

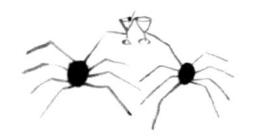

Oh Spider!

Oh Spider, I know you need somewhere to mate,
In Autumn for you it's compelling!
Ambience, atmosphere, a secluded spot
To procreate, reproduce, feel love swelling.

But a word of caution before you enter my space,
To warn you of what will transpire,
For my fear of your presence, your essence, your shape
Will cause consequences so dire.

I've tried overcoming this paranoia, this fear,
Used logic, hypnosis, psychology,
But still you remain my one nemesis
And your demise an inevitability.

Living with OCDN

(Obsessional, Compulsive Disorder – Neatness)

He can spot an errant teaspoon

At a hundred metre paces,

Don't even think about a daring, dirty plate.

Every item, by tradition,

Has its household position

And the crucial need for order is not open for debate.

There's a frisson of despair

If the dishwasher care

Is tardy and the load unrinsed, unclean;

For item placement needs precision

Which means calculated decisions

To fulfil all his crockery fantasies and dreams.

The car is a sacred place, immaculate, pristine,

And on entering this holy place

Keep all thoughts and actions clean.

The boot is not your territory,

For micro planning's necessary

With journeys executed as in a military routine.

But the essence of this philosophy

Is captured in the garden

In a revered and very special place.

For it's the shed that holds the key

To ordered, calm tranquillity

With every screw in a labelled, chosen place.

There are some consequences

When living with this disorder,

This desire for structure, neatness and control,

The immediate reaction

For complete satisfaction

Is blessed chaos when finally alone.

On Clearing Mum's House

We clear your house

We clear your world,

Dismantle the domestic fiefdom

Where you held sway.

Not truly believing this day -

Has come.

We wish we'd listened better

When you'd told us stuff,

Like Grandpa and the war and that aunt who drank enough

To sink a battleship.

We must piece things together and fill in the gaps -

Find the diaries, find the letters

These memories cannot lapse.

So, we assume a tough persona,

Become a Mr. Spock,

Enter an emotional void

And so, begin, take stock.

We wrap and pack and load and know

That each disappearance

Sees an emptiness grow -

In house and hearts.

Longer than we thought,

Though we speeded up - perhaps,

Became increasingly gung-ho,

Now we wearily collapse;

Acknowledge the truth - we can no longer suppress -

The yearnings of our inner child

Who longs to save this nest.

Yoga Class ... *Don't Forget to Breathe ...*

Grab your mat and cushion

Watch the time.

You need to be early

To get your space,

For position is important.

Don't forget to breathe ...

Not at the front

Too obtrusive (think bum),

Not too far back

Might miss a nuanced move.

Sort of ... room-middle-ish.

Don't forget to breathe ...

You bond with your yoga comrades

Your teacher, your yogi, lithe and slender

Who bends and twists,

Like a willow or silver birch.

Effortless.

Don't forget to breathe ...

We follow, effortful,

But dogged and determined.

More sturdy oak than willow

But praised, we glow.

Perhaps we have willow potential.

Don't forget to breathe …

And now drawing to an end it's Shavasana,

Warm and womb-like we lie

Soothed by our yogi's even voice, until

Roused by a shy bell we sit up

Cross our legs and Namaste.

Don't forget to breathe …

Sarah, Our Surprise

Life will go from colour
To black and white without you;
For your love,
Your spirit,
Your enthusiasm,
Are the colours of our world with you.

Life will go from warm to cold
Without your humour,
Your telling of events,
Fast, funny, animated.
Your masterful mispronunciations,
Your creative spelling.
Without your sense of justice, your core of inner strength
That allows you to stand alone.
Life will be colder.

Life, for you, is your family.

For them you've held everything together

Through your strength and courage,

Through the simple *tours de force* of your personality.

You've shown us how to be.

Life for you is your friends – you inspire loyalty.

For those friends and for us,

Each moment now is memorable, precious.

Deceivingly, deceptively, you are still you,

So, we momentarily forget and we smile and laugh and talk.

We remember – and our fury at this unfairness prevails.

There is no compensation for our loss of you;

But as we creak into old age,

You will remain forever beautiful.

Notes

Example: Is a coathanger a suitable choice?

Pros	Cons
Widely available	*May get bent*